I'm Just Sayin'

I'm Just Sayin'
*
A Poetry Anthology for Life Moments

Written by: The Refined Poet

I'm Just Sayin'
A Poetry Anthology for Life Moments

All Rights reserved ©2012 by The Refined Poet

No part of this book may be reproduced or transmitted in any form or by any means, graphic, electronic, or mechanical, including photocopying, recording, taping, or by any information storage or retrieval system, without the permission in writing from the publisher.

Front & Back Cover Designs by Abundant Truth Publishing

Abundant Truth Publishing
an imprint of Abundant Truth International Ministries

For information address:
Abundant Truth International
P.O. Box 126
Camden, NC 27921

Unless otherwise indicated, all of the scripture quotations are taken from the *Authorized King James Version* **of the Bible. Scripture quotations marked with NIV are taken from the** *New International Version* **of the Bible. Scripture quotations marked with ASV are taken from the** *American Standard Version* **of the Bible. Scripture quotations marked with GW are taken from the** *God's Word Bible.*

ISBN 13: 978-1-60141-614-8

Printed in the United States of America.

Contents

Preface

Introduction

Section 1 – Moments of Pain   1

Lost (Villanelle Style)   3
Scream and Howl   7
No Words   11
Broken Heart   15
Torture   19

Section 2 – Moments of Introspection   23

Refreshing Spring (Japanese Tanka)   25
Inspiration   29
Quicken Me   33
In Honor of Love (Terza Rima Sonnet)   37
The Meadows   41
In Praise of Amelia   45

Section 3 – Moments of Madness   49

Anguish   51
Misunderstood   55
Piece of My Mind   59

Contents (cont.)

The Successful Failure	63
I Know the Truth	67

Just for fun...   **71**

Sleepy, Weepy, Me	73
Little Jenny's Fire Sale	77
My Cat	81
The Never-Ending Hangover	85

About the Author   **89**

My Poetic Prose   **91**

Preface

I hope the poems of this anthology will encourage and inspire. I create poetry under the pseudonym of "The Refined Poet" due to the style of my writings.

I do not write from a place of angst, frustration, or inner turmoil. My poetry comes from biblical, thoughtful introspection and consideration of various topics while respecting the many forms of the poetic genre. Hope you enjoy this collection. – TRP

Introduction

Have you ever had a "moment?" Sure you have. We've all experienced events in life that preceded these moments of confusion, explosion, and even bliss. The poems presented in this anthology express feelings and thoughts accompanying these life moments.

SANCTUARY FOR THE SOUL

A Poetical Anthology for Life's Journey

-Section 1-
~Moments of Pain~
(Poems Reflecting on Times of Emotional Pain)

SANCTUARY FOR THE SOUL
A Poetical Anthology for Life's Journey

Inspiration: *This poetic piece reflects on times of despair following a bad break up.*
~TRP~

SANCTUARY FOR THE SOUL
A Poetical Anthology for Life's Journey

~*Lost*~
(Villanelle Style)

I am lost as a ship at sea,
Tossed by waves of pain and hurt.
How could this happen to me?

Your lies did deceive,
Such tales your mouth did spurt!
I am lost as a ship at sea

A shadow of the person I used to be,
I have lost all sense of personal worth.
How could this happen to me?

I still cannot grasp and believe;
Anger covers me as sand on the earth.
I am lost as a ship at sea

Brake up or break up? It's both you see;
Love stopped, lives divided if by a curse.

SANCTUARY FOR THE SOUL
A Poetical Anthology for Life's Journey

How could this happen to me?

I will never love again or be free,
For devastation has performed its work

I am lost as a ship at sea,
How could this happen to me

SANCTUARY FOR THE SOUL
A Poetical Anthology for Life's Journey

My Reflections

SANCTUARY FOR THE SOUL
A Poetical Anthology for Life's Journey

Inspiration: This poetic piece demonstrates social and personal angst. We come into the world crying, We go through growing pains. We transition into finding ourselves, all the while, trying to leave our mark on the world.
~TRP~

SANCTUARY FOR THE SOUL

A Poetical Anthology for Life's Journey

~*Scream and Howl*~

Enter the world by a scream and howl.
Doctor, why the pain at my existence?
As I grow I howl, yell, and moan.
Will this never end?

My teeth crack and become undone,
As time ravages my body.
My skin bursts with sores,
Rising and falling at will.

My heart screams and howls,
How could it be battered?
Love should not be so cruel.
My cry goes on into the night.

Life goes on.
I learn. I study.

SANCTUARY FOR THE SOUL
A Poetical Anthology for Life's Journey

I howl for freedom.
Yet, I become a slave to the system.

Hear ye, hear me! I matter!
Howl ye, howl with me!
Let us change the world.

The view must change
The laws must change.
Howl until the world knows your name!
Enter the world by a scream and howl,
Leave it shaken, battered, calling your name!

My Reflections

SANCTUARY FOR THE SOUL
A Poetical Anthology for Life's Journey

Inspiration: *This poetic piece expresses mixed, painful feelings of loss, love, abandonment, and breakup. Sometimes, your emotions are in conflict that you have so much to say, but end up not saying a word.*
~TRP~

~No Words~

D*eciding before I go,*

W*hich emotions I will show...*

P*ain?*

L*ove?*

D*iscomfort?*

F*ear or dread?*

D*eparted, no words said.*

SANCTUARY FOR THE SOUL
A Poetical Anthology for Life's Journey

My Reflections

My Reflections

SANCTUARY FOR THE SOUL
A Poetical Anthology for Life's Journey

Inspiration: *This poetic piece expresses the pain of heartbreak and love which was lost.*
~TRP~

~Broken Heart~

My heart fell apart.
Words pierced it
Splitting it asunder
No repairman in sight

My heart broken
Pain fills it
Making it hard to breathe
No physician on call

My heart aching
Sorrow takes hold
Grieving the mind and soul
No consolation found

SANCTUARY FOR THE SOUL
A Poetical Anthology for Life's Journey

My Reflections

My Reflections

Inspiration: *This poetic piece describes the torment of one-sided relationships, where the feelings of one of the participants are hard to understand. ~TRP~*

SANCTUARY FOR THE SOUL
A Poetical Anthology for Life's Journey

~*Torture*~

The torment fills me
The pain grips me,
when you're near me.
Why come close to me?

Your words ensnare me.
Your actions deter me.
Your ways confuse me.
What do you want from me?

You say you love me.
You declare you need me-
You're lost without me.
When will you commit to me?

Torture is what you do to me.
Despair is when you touch me.

SANCTUARY FOR THE SOUL
A Poetical Anthology for Life's Journey

Pain is who you've become to me.

in Loneliness is how you leave me.

SANCTUARY FOR THE SOUL
A Poetical Anthology for Life's Journey

My Reflections

SANCTUARY FOR THE SOUL
A Poetical Anthology for Life's Journey

SANCTUARY FOR THE SOUL

A Poetical Anthology for Life's Journey

-Section 2-
~Moments of Introspection~
(Poems of Contemplation about Nature /Love)

SANCTUARY FOR THE SOUL
A Poetical Anthology for Life's Journey

Inspiration: *This poetic piece inspired by the changing of the season from winter to spring*
~TRP~

SANCTUARY FOR THE SOUL

A Poetical Anthology for Life's Journey

~*Refreshing Spring*~
(Japanese Tanka)

The dew falls gently

Rain gives new life to the earth

Heavy hearts made glad

A new season flourishes

Tranquility, peace renewed

SANCTUARY FOR THE SOUL
A Poetical Anthology for Life's Journey

My Reflections

SANCTUARY FOR THE SOUL
A Poetical Anthology for Life's Journey

My Reflections

SANCTUARY FOR THE SOUL
A Poetical Anthology for Life's Journey

Inspiration: *This poetic piece describes the inspiration that is found in fruitful relationships, whether familial, romantic, or friendly. ~TRP~*

~*Inspiration*~

Your presence radiates such peace.

The joy in your eyes brightens my soul.

Your words gently soothe my mind.

You bring heaven down to earth.

Inspiration, you are to me.

My Reflections

My Reflections

SANCTUARY FOR THE SOUL
A Poetical Anthology for Life's Journey

***Inspiration:** This poetic piece reflects on one's longing for companionship and the rekindling of an old romantic relationship. ~TRP~*

~Quicken Me~

Quicken me again in your embrace

Make the world dissolve around us

I will live again

I will love again

SANCTUARY FOR THE SOUL
A Poetical Anthology for Life's Journey

My Reflections

My Reflections

SANCTUARY FOR THE SOUL
A Poetical Anthology for Life's Journey

Inspiration: *This poetic piece reflects appreciation for love itself. ~TRP~*

SANCTUARY FOR THE SOUL
A Poetical Anthology for Life's Journey

~*In Honor of Love*~
(Terza Rima Sonnet)

Love, thou greatest of all pious virtues;
For you do men wander the streets and halls.
Women sacrifice morals for your truth.

Who ignores your unyielding siren call?
Hearts and souls collide mesmerized by thee;
Destiny shipwrecked, desire is all.

A moment with you, worth more than rubies.
Precious jewels can't stand up against your worth.
Despite pains, your quest... a call of duty.

SANCTUARY FOR THE SOUL
A Poetical Anthology for Life's Journey

For even brief moments of gladness, mirth,
Men seek your intoxication like brew.
The soul made glad, the heart swells to its girth.

Love, thou art loved, heaven-extolled are you.
You give life meaning, revealing what's true.

SANCTUARY FOR THE SOUL
A Poetical Anthology for Life's Journey

My Reflections

SANCTUARY FOR THE SOUL
A Poetical Anthology for Life's Journey

Inspiration: *This poetic piece reflects a youth's memories of love, freedom, and peaceful plains. ~TRP~*

~The Meadows~

How I long for the meadows
Where nature rules in quiet stillness
Refreshing, Reviving, Replenishing
all who adore the wilderness

How I long for the meadows
where true love was discovered
Inviting, Inciting, Instilling
desires not to be smothered

How I long for the meadows
where I was young and free
Laughing, Living, Loving
without any place to be

My Reflections

SANCTUARY FOR THE SOUL

A Poetical Anthology for Life's Journey

My Reflections

SANCTUARY FOR THE SOUL
A Poetical Anthology for Life's Journey

Inspiration: *This poetic piece describes the virtues of the name Amelia. ~TRP~*

SANCTUARY FOR THE SOUL

A Poetical Anthology for Life's Journey

~In Praise of Amelia~

Surely the flower stamped by you,

Endures shifts of seasons through and through.

The woman who holds your name,

Holds an enduring legacy soaring above the plains.

All who hear the syllables of your form,

Will be compelled to see beauty in all who are born

My Reflections

My Reflections

SANCTUARY FOR THE SOUL
A Poetical Anthology for Life's Journey

SANCTUARY FOR THE SOUL
A Poetical Anthology for Life's Journey

-Section 3-
~Moments of Madness~
(Poems Expressing Moments of Mental Turmoil)

SANCTUARY FOR THE SOUL
A Poetical Anthology for Life's Journey

Inspiration: *This poetic piece describes the challenge to remain calm after being angered. The desire to maintain self-control can be tested greatly. ~TRP~*

~Anguish~

Like a cord stretched to the point of breaking
Unstable as a building after a quaking
My emotions have awakened from rest
Forming as violent winds headed west

I now know why lions roar
And bears at times attack
When safety and comfort is lost
It reveals the need to fight back

Yet I am no lion, neither a bear
Whose ways are vicious and primal
I have reason and intellect

Keeping me from being vengeful and homicidal

The need for release is growing within me
But the ensuing carnage must not be
Hence I am left to bemoan and languish
Sitting here now full of rage and anguish

My Reflections

Inspiration: *This poetic piece probes how we respond to and deal with being misunderstood. ~TRP~*

~Misunderstood~

How I hate being misunderstood!

Efforts of others simply are no good.

Offering with concern their advice,

I nod in acceptance to be nice.

My Reflections

My Reflections

SANCTUARY FOR THE SOUL
A Poetical Anthology for Life's Journey

Inspiration: *This poetic piece expresses feelings of frustration from being misunderstood and the resolve to set the record straight. ~TRP~*

~Piece of My Mind~

I have held my peace long enough;
Tired of the drama and stupid stuff!
Silence, I thought, was the path to peace,
Yet, you continue your discourse with no relief.

Since you fail to come to your senses,
It is my job to help mend fences.
My words will be brief, concise, and true.
Tired of the drama, and at this point; also of you.

If my words fail to bring a truce,
It will not deter me from the truth.
You got it all wrong, this is certain,
But I'm the only one bearing this burden.

SANCTUARY FOR THE SOUL
A Poetical Anthology for Life's Journey

***I** will free myself from silence which is called "golden,"*
And end this conflict which is now boring.
Silence, I thought, was the path to peace,
Yet, you continue your discourse with no relief.
***W**anted to get out of this with grace this time.*
Since you asked for it -

A PIECE OF MY MIND!

My Reflections

SANCTUARY FOR THE SOUL
A Poetical Anthology for Life's Journey

Inspiration: *This poetic piece shows how depression and defeat can become permanent attitudes when one experiences repeat failures. ~TRP~*

SANCTUARY FOR THE SOUL

A Poetical Anthology for Life's Journey

~*The Successful Failure*~

Like water spilling on the ground
Absorbed, never to be seen again
Such has been the flow of my life.

In my hands, greatness.
In my grasp, fulfillment.
But what?
Let it slip as a full glass,
Feeling splashes of regret, pain, sorrow.

The glass of hope shattered;
Expectation of good things spilled.

Will I ever get up again?
Should I fill life's glass with anticipation?

Will I try once more to refresh my vessel
with feats unknown?
It now sits on the shelf.

The only success I achieve... Failure!

My Reflections

SANCTUARY FOR THE SOUL
A Poetical Anthology for Life's Journey

Inspiration: *This poetic piece expresses the effects of social phobia and anxiety that we all experience to varying degrees. This poem details the thoughts of someone paranoid about simply using the restroom in public.*
~TRP~

~I Know the Truth~

Decisions. Doubts. Despair.
Why are these my friends and foes?

Caught between holding on and letting go.
All of my fears will pass
if I go through this door.
It's only steps away,
But their eyes are already on me.
They pretend not to notice me,
Yet I know the truth.

Problems with my appearance.
Judging my stance.
Evaluating my walk.
I am the topic of everyone's conversation.

Caught between holding on and letting go.

All of my frustrations will pass if I get to the door.
Steps seem like miles,
Their eyes piercing.
Their thoughts probing.

What will he do?
How long will he take?
They pretend not to be aware of my presence,
I know the truth.

Nature is calling.
Fear is yelling.
That which sounds louder will always win.
If my choice is a sin, it is mine alone.

Well, it is decided.
Fear wins again.

Can't get up to go to the bathroom. But why?

Their eyes piercing.

Their thoughts probing.

I am convinced of this truth.

My dilemma ends again.

My Reflections

~JUST FOR FUN...~

The poems in this section are exercises in humor and poetic fun.

SANCTUARY FOR THE SOUL
A Poetical Anthology for Life's Journey

Inspiration: *I wrote this poem late one night while not being able to sleep. Personally, a fun write. ~TRP~*

SANCTUARY FOR THE SOUL

A Poetical Anthology for Life's Journey

~Sleepy, Weepy, Me~

Gosh, I am so sleepy!

Why am I still up?

It's as if I had nothing else to do,

But lay here stuck in a rut.

Weeping on the inside,

Cause I am not finding sleep on the outside.

Nothing to watch

Nothing to eat

Still looking for that gift of sleep.

Well, let's see if writing helps.

As I type some alertness left.

Hope I finish this poem,

For I no longer want to weep.

My eyes are now heavy,

Yes sir! It's time for me to sleep.

SANCTUARY FOR THE SOUL
A Poetical Anthology for Life's Journey

My Reflections

SANCTUARY FOR THE SOUL
A Poetical Anthology for Life's Journey

Inspiration: *I wrote this poem as homage to the proverbial new child. ~TRP~*

SANCTUARY FOR THE SOUL
A Poetical Anthology for Life's Journey

~*Little Jenny's Fire Sale*~

The doctor... I mean salesman told me,
"Once the baby is out of the womb,
its value goes down instantly."
Now, who wants a used baby?

I know it's a cliché -
The firstborn not wanting
the new kid to stay
But hey, what am I to do?
I just don't think
there is room enough for two.

What's the problem - It seems I can't make a dime.
Maybe I need to develop a slogan with a rhyme:

*"We specialize in pre-owned little brothers,
fits any size family, with or without a
mother!"*

*I guess if I must keep him
I will cry and scream now
He may come to my rescue one day,
then, only then, will he make me proud.*

SANCTUARY FOR THE SOUL
A Poetical Anthology for Life's Journey

My Reflections

SANCTUARY FOR THE SOUL
A Poetical Anthology for Life's Journey

Inspiration: *In honor of all my cartoon cat heroes. ~TRP~*

SANCTUARY FOR THE SOUL
A Poetical Anthology for Life's Journey

~My Cat~

*My cat is not like **Felix***

She does not perform magic tricks

*My cat is not like **Sylvester***

She does not talk with a lisp

*My cat is not like **Garfield***

She does not use the postal system

*My cat is not like **Tom***

She does not chase a mouse like she's mental

My cat is just a cat.

The Refined Poet

My Reflections

My Reflections

SANCTUARY FOR THE SOUL
A Poetical Anthology for Life's Journey

Inspiration: *I wrote this poem for a contest. You decide. ~TRP~*

~*The Never-ending Hangover*~

I arise today with veiled memories.
Was it a dream, reality, or hallucinations?
Just can't decide due to the "libations."

What did I say?
Did I drink?
What did I do?
Can someone tell me,
Why I am feeling regrets anew?

Wait a minute!
What time is it?
Oh wow, it is well past 9.
Shouldn't I be a work, isn't it time?

Then, I remembered what libation I had,
On the previous day that led me to this place
that I am.

It wasn't alcohol, beer, or wine,
But its taste still gives me a buzz even now.

I have a hangover that will never end,
It's because of freedom from a job that was worse than sin.
Yes! I did quit!
Yes! I said I wouldn't go back.
Now I lay here intoxicated with the libation of freedom in fact.

No place to go.
No place to be.
I will worry about bills later.
But now as I rollover,
I hope this is the start of a never-ending hangover.

My Reflections

My Reflections

~About the Author~

The Refined Poet is a poet, psalmist, author, and minister. He has written numerous poems, books, articles, blogs, teaching resources, devotional materials, and music for the Christian community.

His poetry reflects sound, biblical Christian thought, encouraging those of the Christian faith. His versatility in poetic prose provides inspiration for those who appreciate the poetry genre. His motto for his poetry is: "Write to Inspire. Write to Express. Write to Live."

I create poetry under the pseudonym of "The Refined Poet" due to the style of my writings. I do not write from a place of angst, frustration, or inner turmoil. My poetry comes from biblical, thoughtful introspection and consideration of various topics while respecting the many forms of the poetic genre. ~TRP~

SANCTUARY FOR THE SOUL
A Poetical Anthology for Life's Journey

For more poetry, please visit The Refined Poet online at therefinedpoet.net

My Poetic Prose

SANCTUARY FOR THE SOUL
A Poetical Anthology for Life's Journey

"In this section, I invite you to try creating some poetry of your own."

SANCTUARY FOR THE SOUL
A Poetical Anthology for Life's Journey

My Poetic Prose

_____

_____

_____

_____

_____

_____

_____

_____

_____

_____

_____

_____

_____

_____

_____

_____

_____

SANCTUARY FOR THE SOUL
A Poetical Anthology for Life's Journey

My Poetic Prose

My Poetic Prose

My Poetic Prose

My Poetic Prose

My Poetic Prose

SANCTUARY FOR THE SOUL
A Poetical Anthology for Life's Journey

My Poetic Prose

SANCTUARY FOR THE SOUL
A Poetical Anthology for Life's Journey

My Poetic Prose